This book

Sarah and Paul
Have a Visitor

Discover about
The Lord Jesus Christ

Derek Prime

Christian Focus Publications

illustrations
by
Janis Mennie

Published by

CHRISTIAN FOCUS PUBLICATIONS LTD

Houston   **Tain**
Texas   **Ross-shire**

© **1989 Derek Prime**

ISBN 1 871676 19 3

Reprinted 1995

CONTENTS

To Anna, Emily, Deborah and Andrew

1 Robert comes to stay

Very early on Sunday morning the telephone rang. Paul and Sarah MacDonald, who were twins, heard their father go down the stairs to answer it. They guessed by the way he was talking that there was some bad news.

'Yes,' they heard him say, 'we'll be glad for Robert to stay here. Why don't you let him come after church today? Then you can go off early tomorrow morning because you have a long journey ahead of you...Yes. That will be fine.'

Paul and Sarah weren't sure who their father was speaking to. They only knew one Robert and he was the four-year-old son of their parents' friends at church. As their father came up the stairs they couldn't hide their curiosity.

'Dad, we heard you talking about Robert. Was it Robert Tyson?'

'Yes,' answered Mr MacDonald. 'Mr and Mrs Tyson have just received bad news. Mr Tyson's elderly mother died suddenly during the night. Mr Tyson feels that he and his wife must go south to where she lived as soon as possible. He needs to help his father do all the things that have to be done. The Tysons were wondering whether Robert could stay with us for a few days - it might be as long as a week. Of course, I said yes. Robert's coming to us after church. I hope he won't be too home-sick.'

'We'll do our best to help him feel at home,' promised Sarah. 'It will be fun having someone younger to play with. He can play with our toys when we're at school, can't he, Paul?'

'Yes,' nodded Paul. 'I'll get out some of my old toys that I played with when I was younger.'

'Have you remembered that it's Harvest Thanksgiving at church this morning?' Mrs MacDonald asked her husband. 'I took our gifts down to church yesterday afternoon. The children will take theirs with them this morning.'

'I'd forgotten that,' Mr MacDonald said. 'I always find it interesting to see all the different gifts of food and flowers people bring. Have you children got your gifts ready to give to your Sunday School teacher?'

'I've decided to take apples, oranges and grapes and I've tied a blue ribbon on the basket, Dad,' explained Sarah. 'Paul's taking tins - baked beans, of course, his favourites. He doesn't want a ribbon on his.'

****

They could tell it was harvest-time as soon as they went through the church doors.

'What a lovely smell!' exclaimed Sarah.

'Doesn't it look good?' added Paul.

There were flowers and vegetables, fruit and tins of all sorts of things. It looked like the inside of a supermarket!

'Look at that large loaf of bread in the middle, Paul. Isn't it huge?'

'Look at that pile of potatoes, too, Sarah.'

Mr and Mrs Tyson and Robert came and sat next to the MacDonalds and together they nearly filled the whole row. The children enjoyed singing the harvest hymns, especially their favourite one, 'We plough the fields and scatter the good seed on the land...' Robert couldn't read yet, but he knew the chorus, 'All good gifts around us,' and he joined in very loudly when the time came to sing it.

****

During the afternoon Robert didn't seem unhappy about leaving his parents. He liked being with Paul and Sarah, as they played with him and read him stories.

After supper Mrs MacDonald explained to Robert about his bedtime. 'I think you must go up to bed now, Robert, as it's eight o'clock, and your mummy said that was your usual time.'

'Will the twins come to bed, too?' Robert asked, a hint of tears coming to his eyes.

'No, not just yet. They'll go a little later because they're older.'

'I don't want to go to bed on my own,' complained Robert, sounding very tearful.

'I'll tell you what,' said Sarah. 'Mum will read you a Bible story before you go to bed and Paul and I will come up with you and listen to it. How would that be?'

Robert nodded his head in approval.

'Get undressed first then, Robert, and as soon as you're washed and in your pyjamas, we'll have the story in your bedroom.'

The story Robert chose was the feeding of the five thousand with the little boy's lunch of loaves and fishes. When Mrs MacDonald had finished reading it she said, 'That was a good story to choose, Robert, on Harvest Sunday! Making the loaves and fishes go such a long way is what we call a miracle. It was easy for the Lord Jesus to do because He's God, and He made everything.'

'Yes,' added Sarah, 'in Sunday School this morning we were told that the Lord Jesus made all the food and flowers we could see in church.'

'Did Jesus make everything?' asked Robert.

'Yes, everything. All the wonderful gifts we see at harvest were made by the Lord Jesus Christ.'

Mrs MacDonald remembered Robert's singing in the morning service. 'Let's sing "All Good Gifts," shall we?'

A big smile came on Robert's face as they sang together -

'All good gifts around us
Are sent from heaven above;
Then thank the Lord, O thank the Lord,
For all His love.'

'I like singing,' Robert said. 'Can we sing again?'

'Yes, of course. We'll sing again in a minute.'

Robert thought for a moment, and then said, 'What does Jesus look like?'

'I don't really know,' answered Mrs MacDonald.

'I do,' explained Robert. 'I've seen a picture of Him at Sunday School.'

'That's only a drawing, silly,' interrupted Paul.

'No, he isn't silly, Paul,' Mrs MacDonald corrected. 'Robert is quite right. Many artists have drawn pictures of the Lord Jesus and you can see them in storybooks. But you must remember that the artists are only guessing what Jesus looks like.'

'I'm sure He looks very kind,' added Sarah. 'The sort of person I'd like to have as a friend.'

'You're right, Sarah,' agreed her mother. 'The Bible doesn't give us a photograph of Jesus. Instead it does something much better - it tells us the kind of person the Lord Jesus is. It tells us He is perfect, loving and kind - the best Friend a boy or girl can have. Who's your best friend at school, Paul?'

Paul thought for a moment. 'I suppose Philip or Chris. Yes, I'd put Chris first.'

'Why is he your very best friend?'

'He's such a good friend. He shares things; he never lets you down; and he likes doing the same things I do.'

'It isn't because of what he looks like then that he's your best friend?'

'Of course not!' exclaimed Paul. 'That doesn't matter.'

'Then you can see why the Bible doesn't tell us what the Lord Jesus looks like,' continued Mrs MacDonald, 'but instead tells us the kind of person He is. He's the most wonderful Person who has ever lived on this earth. He was always kind. He never let anyone down. He willingly died to save His friends.'

'We'll see Jesus one day though, won't we? When He comes again? The Bible says so.'

'Yes, Sarah,' agreed her mother, 'and that will be a wonderful day.'

Mrs MacDonald looked at Robert and noticed how tired he was looking. 'Into bed, sleepy-head!'

When Robert had climbed into bed, he looked a little unhappy. Sarah and Paul guessed that he was missing his own home and parents. Mrs MacDonald helped Robert to say his prayers. They asked the Lord Jesus to keep Robert safe until the morning and to bless his parents as they helped his grand-dad.

Mrs MacDonald was just about to switch off the light when Robert asked, 'If we close the curtains, Jesus can't see me, can He?'

She smiled. 'Yes, He can, Robert. The Lord Jesus is God and He sees and knows everything. Nothing happens anywhere without His knowing all about it. Because of this He's able to keep us safe. He sees me and He sees Paul and Sarah, and He sees your mummy and daddy too. And He watches over us all. He never wants us to be lonely. He always stays with us.'

'Even when we've been naughty and disobedient,' added Sarah.

'Yes and no, Sarah. The Lord Jesus doesn't leave us, but we don't please Him when we sin. If we're truly sorry He will forgive us, and help us to do better. The

Lord Jesus is the best Friend you can have. He will always stay close to you.'

'I know a chorus about that,' Robert said.

'So do we,' Paul and Sarah chimed in together.

'All right,' suggested Mrs MacDonald, 'let's sing it before we say good night.'

Jesus is with me all through the night,
Stays close beside me all through the
night,
So I sleep safely till morning light,
Jesus is with me all through the night.'

'Good night, Robert. I'll buy you a Bible colouring book tomorrow morning. You can colour it while the twins are at school, and we'll talk about the pictures with the twins at bedtime.'

'Good night,' said the twins.

'Good night,' said a little voice under the covers and in no time Robert was asleep.

2 Robert gets his book

'There they are, Robert!' called out Mrs MacDonald as first there was a ring at the doorbell and then a loud rat-a-tat. 'Only the twins could make all that noise!'

Robert ran excitedly to the front door. He'd been waiting impatiently nearly all afternoon for Sarah and Paul to come home from school. He couldn't reach the lock on the front door, so he had to wait for Mrs MacDonald to come and open it.

'Hello Robert,' said Sarah, as she put down her schoolbag in the hall. 'Have you been playing with our toys?' Robert nodded his head.

'Yes, he has,' said Mrs MacDonald. 'He had Paul's train out this morning.'

'Not my electric one?' asked Paul, who felt that Robert was rather young to play with his electric train on his own.

'Oh, no,' answered his mother. 'We found the old clock-work train and rails. Then he played with your fort and Sarah's dolls house.'

'Better than going to school!' exclaimed Paul.

'He also helped me hang out the washing,'

went on Mrs MacDonald. 'But how about you two? I expect you're hungry. What did you have for lunch today?'

'Sausages again,' replied Sarah, 'and lemon tart afterward.'

'A snack is ready on the table. Robert will sit at the opposite end to me and you two on either side. When we've had our snack I've promised Sarah I'll go with her next door to take a small present for Mrs Brown's new baby. She and her baby daughter only came out of hospital the day before yesterday. You'll look after Robert for a few minutes, won't you, Paul?'

****

Sarah was quite excited about seeing the new baby. She wondered if perhaps she might be a nurse when she left school and learn how to look after mothers and their babies.

'In biology at school, Mum, we've been studying how we're born. I'm glad you told Paul and me all about it when Auntie Anne had her baby. It's all rather wonderful, isn't it?'

'Yes,' her mother agreed with a smile.

16

'Now remember if Mrs Brown invites us in, we mustn't stay more than a few minutes because she will have lots to do in these first days home.'

Mrs Brown came to the door when they rang the bell, and immediately took them into the front room to see the baby.

'What's her name?' asked Sarah.

'Susan,' replied Mrs Brown. 'Would you like to hold her?'

'Yes, please!'

'You are privileged!' said her mother.

****

When Sarah and Mrs MacDonald came back home Paul was showing Robert his electric train.

Sarah remembered her mother's promise. 'Did Mum buy you a Bible colouring book, Robert?'

'Yes, would you like to see it?'

'Yes, please.'

Robert turned over the first pages of his colouring book and showed them to Sarah and Paul.

'I did three pictures this afternoon.'

Paul looked closely and rather critically at the colouring of one picture. 'You didn't keep in the lines very well there.'

'Neither did you when you were four!' interrupted his mother from the kitchen, where she was washing the dishes after their snack.

'Look,' urged Sarah, 'he did that one nicely.'

The picture was of the stable at Bethlehem. Mary and Joseph were on one side of the picture, and in Mary's lap was the baby Jesus. Next to Mary was the manger the baby Jesus was to be laid in. On the other side of the picture there were shepherds.

Mrs MacDonald came and sat down with the twins and Robert. 'Tell us who all the people are, Robert,' she suggested.

'That's Mary in the blue; and Joseph is standing next to her.'

'Who are the people visiting them?'

'The shepherds.'

Across the top of the picture there was the word Emmanuel to be coloured in, and underneath in small letters the words 'God with us.' Robert had coloured 'Emmanuel' in red and the words underneath in yellow.

Paul looked at his mother and asked, 'Why is "God with us" under the word "Emmanuel"?'

'Oh, because that's what the word "Emmanuel" means. You'll find it in the first chapter of St. Matthew's Gospel. Run upstairs and get your Bible and you can see.'

In half a minute Paul was back, having found chapter one on his way downstairs. 'I've found it,' he said. 'Verses twenty-two and twenty-three: "All this took place to fulfil what the Lord had said through the prophet: The virgin will be with child and will give birth to a son, and they will call him Emmanuel - which means, God with us."'

Mrs MacDonald nodded her head. 'The prophet Isaiah said all this would happen many years before.'

'Did the prophets know all about Jesus coming?' asked Sarah.

'Yes: they were like look-out men,' explained Mrs MacDonald.

'I put look-out men in the towers on Paul's fort,' interrupted Robert.

Mrs MacDonald smiled. 'The prophets were looking out for the Messiah, the Christ. They wanted to tell God's people that He

was going to come and what He was going to do. They knew that He would be more than just a man. They spoke of Him as being both God and man.'

Paul knew that Jesus became a man, and he knew that He is God, but he didn't understand it very well. 'How do we know that Jesus is God and man? It happened such a long time ago, didn't it?'

'Well,' began Mrs MacDonald thoughtfully, 'you've just read what the Prophet Isaiah said, that the Lord Jesus would be "God with us". And another prophet called Micah said that the Christ who was going to be born as a human baby in Bethlehem had always existed. So he knew that Christ would be both God and man.'

Paul had read in his comics about supermen. 'Was Jesus a kind of superman?'

'Definitely not,' replied Mrs MacDonald. 'He was really a man and He was really God - at the same time. The Bible doesn't explain this because it's too difficult for us to understand. But it tells us that it's true. The disciples knew it was. Jesus was a man - there was no doubt about that. They met Him just like other men, and they got to know Him well. Then they discovered that He was God. Everything they saw about the Lord Jesus made them realise that He was God's Son.'

Sarah had been thinking about Robert's picture. 'Is that why His birth was different? Joseph wasn't really Jesus' father, was he?'

'No,' agreed Mrs MacDonald. 'You've been learning at school how we're born, and Sarah reminded me of how I explained it to you when Auntie Anne's baby was born.'

'Yes, I remember,' nodded Paul.

'Good,' Mrs MacDonald went on. 'The Lord Jesus' human life began inside Mary by a miracle performed by the Holy Spirit, so that He had no human father, only a human mother.'

Paul remembered how once he had had to pretend he was an angel in a nativity play at school, so he asked, 'It wasn't make-believe, was it? Jesus didn't just dress up as a man?'

'Oh, no. He grew up as a boy, just like you. Look at Robert's picture.'

Robert had become rather bored with listening to what the twins and Mrs

MacDonald were talking about, because he couldn't understand. He had started colouring the fourth picture in his book. It was a drawing of Jesus in the temple at Jerusalem asking questions.

Mrs MacDonald went on. 'The Lord Jesus liked asking questions as a boy, just like you do. He was sometimes tired and thirsty. He was like us in every way, except for one thing. Do you know what that was?'

Sarah answered first. 'Jesus never did anything wrong.'

Paul had been thinking hard about all that had been said. 'There must have been a very important reason for Jesus to become a man.'

'Yes,' agreed his mother, 'only someone who was perfect could die in the place of people who have done wrong in order to take away their sin. There wasn't a man good enough to do it. You know why, don't you? Sarah hinted at it just now.'

'We've all done things wrong,' answered Paul.

'But how do you know that everyone everywhere has done wrong things?' asked Sarah.

Her mother smiled. 'First of all, the Bible tells us so. And then we know we've sinned. You have, haven't you?'

Paul and Sarah nodded.

'What about you, Robert? Have you ever been disobedient and naughty?'

Robert looked a little ashamed.

'Oh, don't look so miserable,' Mrs MacDonald said with a laugh. 'I'm not going to tell you off! But you see our sin shows how much we need a Saviour. Being God and being a perfect man, the Lord Jesus was able to die for sinners, so they could be forgiven.'

Robert had finished the picture of Jesus in the temple now. It was by far the best he had done.

'You've coloured that very well, Robert,' congratulated Mrs MacDonald.

Sarah looked at Paul. 'Shall we have a game with Robert?'

'Yes; what?'

'I spy with my little eye.'

'All right, that's a good idea. Are you ready, Robert? I spy with my little eye something beginning with t.'

'I can't spell,' said Robert, with a sob in his voice, for he was nearly in tears.

'Sorry,' apologized Sarah. 'Let's play it with colours then. Start again, Paul, but tell us the colour instead of the first letter.'

3 Letter from Rochester

Sarah was looking out of the window as the MacDonald family and young Robert sat eating their breakfast, when she saw someone coming up the path to their house.

'I think we've got some mail today,' she said.

No sooner had she said this than the doorbell rang.

'May I answer the door, please?' said Paul.

'Yes,' said his father.

Paul ran to the door. There was a small packet for Mr MacDonald, a letter addressed to Mr and Mrs MacDonald, and two postcards. One postcard was addressed to Robert, and the other to Paul and Sarah.

Mr MacDonald looked at the postmark on the letter. 'It's from Robert's parents. Your card looks interesting, Robert.'

'It's a picture of a horse. Can you read, please, what's written on the other side?'

Sarah was sitting next to Robert, so she read what his parents had written. 'We shall be back home soon. Lots of love, Mummy and Daddy.'

Mr MacDonald had been reading Mr and Mrs Tyson's letter. He passed it to his wife and said, 'Robert's Grandma's funeral is to be on Thursday. They hope to be back home on Saturday.'

Robert heard what Mr MacDonald said although he did not understand what a 'funeral' was. He did know, however, that his grandmother had died.

****

In the afternoon Robert went shopping with Mrs MacDonald, before they went to meet Paul and Sarah from school. While they were in the supermarket, Robert asked, 'May I have a lollipop, please?'

Mrs MacDonald laughed. 'All right. You can choose one for yourself and one for each of the twins.'

As they came out of the supermarket four large black cars drove slowly past. Robert liked cars and he collected small model cars.

'Is that a wedding?' he asked.

'No, Robert. It's a funeral.'

'Like Grandma will have on Thursday?'

'Yes, that's right.'

'What are all the flowers for?'

'All the people who knew and loved the person who died show their love by sending flowers,' explained Mrs MacDonald.

'Can I send some for Grandma?'

'Yes, of course, you can, Robert. That would be very kind. "Uncle" David is going to arrange for some flowers to be sent from all of us. He'll put your name on the card that goes with them.'

By the time all Robert's questions had been answered, they were at the school. On the way home Paul and Sarah talked about school and discussed the things they wanted to do with Robert.

When they arrived home, Mrs MacDonald asked, 'Well, what have you decided you'd like to do first?'

'Colouring,' explained Sarah.

Paul added, 'We want to make our own pictures. Then you can judge them. It will be a competition.'

'I can't draw very well,' Robert said.

'You can colour one of the pictures in your Bible colouring book then,' suggested Paul.

Mrs MacDonald agreed that this was a good idea.

Robert's picture was full of people. There was a crowded street with men in some kind of procession. On one side were Jesus and His disciples. Next to Him was a woman with her arms around someone who looked as if he was her son. There were words to be coloured at the top of the picture. The words were: 'Jesus went about doing good.' The title for the picture was at the bottom of the page - 'The Widow of Nain.'

'Shall I tell you the story, Robert?' Mrs MacDonald suggested.

'Please,' replied Robert eagerly.

'The Lord Jesus went to a town called Nain. His disciples were with Him, and lots of other people. As Jesus came near the gate of the town He met a funeral. It wouldn't have been like the one we saw this afternoon. There were no cars then. I don't expect they sent flowers as we do. Men would have carried the dead person on a stretcher - like you see ambulance men using. Lots of people then followed these men to the place where the person was to be buried. The man who had died was his mother's only son. He meant a lot to her because her husband had also died. When the Lord Jesus saw her He was very sorry for her. He knew how much she would miss her son. He said to her, "Don't cry any more." Then He stepped forward and laid His hand on the stretcher. The men carrying it stopped. Then the Lord Jesus said, "Young man, get up!" Do you know what happened next?'

'Did he get up?' Robert asked eagerly.

'Yes; he sat up and began to talk; and the Lord Jesus gave him back to his mother. She was very happy and thankful to the Lord Jesus.'

Robert looked rather thoughtful. 'Why didn't Jesus make Grandma better?'

'I don't know, Robert,' replied Mrs MacDonald. 'The Lord Jesus doesn't tell us the answers to questions like that now. I expect it was because she was very old. We needn't be sorry for her. She loved Jesus, didn't she?'

Robert nodded.

'Then it's better for her to be with the Lord Jesus in heaven. If she had got better, she would still have been weak and old. But with the Lord Jesus she's in the most exciting place anywhere. We don't have to be afraid of dying when we love and trust the Lord Jesus.'

Sarah and Paul had been listening. They were both sitting at the table, drawing and colouring. Paul had started drawing his own picture of the widow of Nain's son being healed.

'Did Jesus heal everyone?'

'No, He didn't, Paul. It was usually when people came to Him, and asked Him to heal them. He healed all kinds of diseases and illness. How many can you think of?'

'The blind and the deaf.'

'And the dumb and the lame.'

'The paralysed.'

'People with leprosy.'

'That's six,' added up Mrs MacDonald. 'And there were many others too.'

'Why didn't Jesus heal everyone?' Paul asked, rather puzzled.

'One reason was that He couldn't be in every place at once and He didn't only come to heal people. You see,' Mrs MacDonald explained, 'He came to teach people about God and what God wanted them to know.'

'But didn't people need to be healed more than they needed to be taught about God?'

'No, not really, Paul. They may have thought so. But their souls - the invisible part of us that lives forever - were more important. Fetch me my Bible, please. It's on the shelf over there, and I will read what it says.'

'May I read it, please?'

'All right, Sarah. Mark chapter two, and read from the beginning of the chapter, please.'

Sarah read the passage: 'A few days later, when Jesus again entered Capernaum, the people heard that He had come home. So many gathered that there was no room left, not even outside the door, and He preached to them. Some men came, bringing to him a paralytic, carried by four of them. Since they could not get him to Jesus because of the crowd, they made an opening in the roof above Jesus and, after digging through it, lowered the mat the paralysed man was lying on.'

'Digging through the roof must have made a mess,' interrupted Paul.

Mrs MacDonald nodded. 'Carry on reading, please, Sarah.'

'When Jesus saw their faith, He said to the paralytic, "Son your sins are forgiven. " Now some teachers of the law were sitting there, thinking to themselves, "Why does this fellow talk like that? He's blaspheming. Who can forgive sins but God alone?" Immediately Jesus knew in His spirit that this was what they were thinking in their hearts, and He said to them, "Why are you thinking these things? Which is easier: to say to the paralytic, 'Your sins are forgiven,' or to say, 'Get up, take your mat and walk'? But that you may know that the Son of Man has authority on earth to forgive sins. . . " He said to the paralytic, "I tell you, get up, take your mat and go home. " He got up, took his mat and walked out in full view of them all. This amazed everyone and they praised God, saying, "We have never seen anything like this!"'

'Good,' commented Mrs MacDonald. 'Now what was wrong with the man?'

'He was paralysed,' answered Paul.

'Do you know what that means, Robert?'

Robert shook his head.

Mrs MacDonald explained. 'It means that he couldn't walk or move on his own. He was crippled. What did the Lord Jesus say first of all to the paralysed man? Did He tell him to stand up right away?'

'No, He told him that his sins were forgiven,' said Sarah. 'Then afterward He told him to get up.'

'That's right. The Lord Jesus did this to teach them a lesson. It's more important to have our sins forgiven than to have our bodies healed. The Lord Jesus knew that to teach God's Word was His first task. He cared too, of course, for people's bodies. He knew though that our bodies die, but our souls live forever. If people believed His words, and obeyed them, their sins would be forgiven by God.'

Sarah nodded her head. 'You told us yesterday that Jesus was really God and man. How do we know that Jesus is God?'

'I've wondered about that too,' Paul said.

'Yes, it's very important,' agreed Mrs MacDonald, looking at Robert's colouring book. The next picture in Robert's colouring book is the Lord Jesus turning water into wine. That was one of the miracles which showed who Jesus was. Let's leave that picture until tomorrow, Robert. And then we'll ask "Uncle" David to answer Sarah's question.'

4 Mr Macdonald joins in

Mrs MacDonald was washing the dishes after lunch. For most of the morning Robert had played with Paul's soldiers and cars. He had not known what to do after lunch. Mrs MacDonald had suggested he should colour the next picture in his book. It was the picture of Jesus at the wedding in Cana, where He turned the water into wine. As a treat she had let him use Sarah's paints. It made a change from ordinary colouring pencils.

'Have you finished the picture yet, Robert?'

'Yes. But I've made a mess with the water. I'm afraid I knocked some over.'

Mrs MacDonald smiled. She remembered Paul and Sarah doing the same when they were Robert's age. She had put plenty of newspaper on the table, so it didn't matter.

'Never mind,' she called out. 'Tidy up and put the painting over by the window to dry. The twins will want to see it.'

'What can I do now?'

'Wait a few minutes and I'll come and play a game with you.'

Mrs MacDonald had rinsed some empty bottles, which reminded her of a game Mr MacDonald had shown the twins after he had been at a teenagers' party. All she needed was one of the bottles and a box of matches.

'Look, Robert,' she explained. 'I'll put this bottle on the floor between us and we take it in turns to put a match on the top of the bottle. The game is to get as many matches on as we can without knocking any off. If you knock any off, you lose the game.'

Robert thought it sounded easy and it was at first. But the more matches they balanced on the mouth of the bottle, the more difficult it became. Mrs MacDonald knocked two off and Robert won the first game. In the following game Robert knocked them off and Mrs MacDonald won.

'This is fun!' exclaimed Robert. 'I'd like to play this with Paul and Sarah.'

They became so good at the game that they used up a whole box of matches without knocking any off.

'What do we do now? Have we both won?'

'No,' explained Mrs MacDonald. 'We have

to take them off one by one! If you knock or take more than one off, you lose.'

Very carefully they took turns in taking one off. It was not long though before Mrs MacDonald knocked three matches off at once.

'You're the winner, Robert. Now, what you would like for a snack?'

'Peanut butter sandwich, please.'

Mrs MacDonald went to the cupboard. 'I'm afraid there isn't any left, Robert.'

Robert looked a little disappointed and Mrs MacDonald wished she had not asked him what he would like.

'Could we buy some when we go and meet the twins?'

'I'm sorry, Robert, but I wasn't going to meet them today,' said Mrs MacDonald.

Just then the telephone rang. Robert soon guessed Mrs MacDonald was talking to her husband. After she had listened to what Mr MacDonald had to say, she said, 'And could you stop at a supermarket for me on your way home, please? Robert would like some peanut butter and we've unfortunately run out. Thanks. Bye.'

Mrs MacDonald looked at Robert. 'Well, Robert, you'll have your peanut butter sandwich after all! "Uncle" David is coming home from work early today. He's going to meet the twins at school as a surprise and he'll buy the peanut butter before he meets them.'

****

Soon after four o'clock the twins arrived home with their father.

'Dad met us!' they shouted.

'Yes; that was a surprise for you. And it's lovely for all of us to have Dad home so early for a change.'

One of the first things they saw as they came into the dining room was Robert's picture by the window, where he had left it to dry.

'That's a good picture, Robert,' commented Mr MacDonald.

'You're going to talk to us about it,' explained Sarah.

'Am I?' asked Mr MacDonald in surprise.

'Yes, Dad,' confirmed Paul. 'We were talking with Mum last night about the picture in the book next to the one Robert has done today. We asked her how we know that Jesus is God.'

Sarah joined in the explanation. 'Mum said that the turning of water into wine was one of the miracles which showed who Jesus was.'

'Yes, that's right,' agreed Mr MacDonald. 'Do you know the story, Robert?'

'Not really.'

'Paul and Sarah, you tell the story first then.'

'There was a wedding in a place called Cana,' Paul began. 'And Jesus was invited to the wedding.'

'And some of His disciples too,' added Sarah.

'Yes, and Mary, Jesus' mother, was there. They ran out of wine at this wedding. So Mary went to Jesus and told Him. I think she expected Him to send one of His disciples to buy some.'

Mr MacDonald interrupted, 'Like Mum running out of peanut butter, and asking me to get some for Robert!'

They all laughed.

'Carry on, Paul.'

'Before Mary went back to the wedding feast, she said to the servants, "Do whatever Jesus tells you to." Now, standing against the wall there were some stone waterpots. I forget how many.'

'Wait a moment, then,' said Mr MacDonald. 'You can see them in Robert's picture. You count them, Robert.'

'One, two, three, four, five, six waterpots!' shouted Robert.

'What happened then, Sarah?' Mr MacDonald asked.

'Jesus told the servants to fill the waterpots with water right up to the brim. Then He told them to take some of the water out of the waterpots and take it into the feast. So they did as He told them.'

'What happened to the water, Robert, do you think?' asked Mr MacDonald.

'Had it turned into wine?'

'Yes; into the very best wine. Finish the story, please, Sarah.'

'The servants took the water into the feast, and the people tasted it. The man in charge of the feast was surprised. It was the best wine he'd ever tasted. So he spoke to the bridegroom. He said, "When people have

43

a party they always give the best wine first, and the poor wine last. But you've kept the best until last." Not one of the guests knew how it had happened. But the servants and Jesus' disciples knew.'

'That's a wonderful story,' added Mr MacDonald when Sarah finished. 'The Lord Jesus did what no one else could do. He could command something to happen and it happened.'

Paul remembered the story of creation he had heard at Sunday school on Harvest Sunday. 'When God made everything, He just spoke and it happened like that, didn't it, Dad?'

'Yes. That's exactly right, Paul. The Lord Jesus showed He could do what only God can do. All the miracles He did showed this. He didn't do them for Himself, but always to help others and to show them who He was. People were amazed at His power - just as they were at the wedding when they found water turned into wine.'

'People were surprised at His teaching too, weren't they, Dad?' Sarah asked, because she remembered reading this in the Bible.

'True. Often the Gospels tell us that. Do

you know what happened once when soldiers were sent to arrest the Lord Jesus?'

'No, Dad.'

'The soldiers found where the Lord Jesus was and went to arrest Him. There was such a large crowd around Him they couldn't easily reach Him, so they had to listen while they waited for the crowd to go home. As they heard Him speaking, His words were very wonderful to them. They felt they couldn't arrest such a good person. So they went back without the Lord Jesus! They got into trouble for it too. "We never heard anyone teach like this before," they said. Things like this all showed that the Lord Jesus is God.'

Paul asked, 'Did Jesus say He was God, Dad?'

'Yes, He did,' replied Mr MacDonald. 'But He didn't say it very often. Instead He said and did things which only God can say and do. There were times when He admitted that He was the Messiah the Jews were waiting for. This was the same as saying that He's God, because the Jews knew the Messiah would have a special relationship to God. The Lord Jesus also said things about

Himself that no ordinary man would say, except perhaps an impostor.'

'What's an "impostor", Dad?'

'Do you know, Paul?'

'Yes, Dad. Someone who pretends to be someone else.'

'Yes,' went on Mr MacDonald, 'The Lord Jesus said some things that we wouldn't dare say. Suppose, Paul, you said, "I'm the best football player in the world." What would people say?'

'They would say I was bigheaded and boasting, and they would know that I wasn't telling the truth.'

'Well, the Lord Jesus said things - far more important than playing football - and there was nothing boastful about it. He told His disciples that He was the Way, the Truth, and the Life, and that no one can come to God the Father without first coming to Him. These were big things to say, but they are true.'

Sarah remembered what her mother had said. 'When we were talking with Mum, she told us that Jesus was like us in everything except for one thing - He never sinned.'

'Quite right. This is another proof that the

Lord Jesus is God. He never sinned. He broke none of the ten commandments. He never disobeyed His Father. He never told lies or was selfish.'

'How do we know for sure, Dad?' asked Paul.

'The disciples who lived with the Lord Jesus said so. When we live with someone we really know what he's like. I remember someone once saying when we were out that you looked "angelic." It was when you were much younger! But I had to say that you weren't always angelic at home!'

'He isn't now either, Dad.'

'Neither are you, Sarah! The disciples lived with the Lord Jesus and knew what He was like. They wrote it down in the Bible many times. We find Him doing things the Bible tells us only God can do and, therefore, we can be sure that He's God.'

Mr MacDonald paused and thought for a moment. 'Is there a picture of the Resurrection of the Lord Jesus in your book, Robert?'

Robert didn't know.

'I'll look for you, Robert,' Paul offered. 'Yes, there is.'

'Good. When you come to that picture, I'll tell you how the Resurrection shows that the Lord Jesus is God. I think that's enough just for now. What would you all like to do?'

Robert had a good idea. 'Can we play a game?'

'Yes, what would you like to play?'

'Can we play the game where we see how many matchsticks we can put on the top of a bottle.'

Paul and Sarah looked puzzled. 'Do you know how to play it, Robert?'

'"Auntie" showed me this afternoon. I'm good at it.'

'Let's see, shall we twins?' asked Mr MacDonald, winking at them.

5 Mr MacDonald brings home a surprise

It was a wet and windy day as the twins walked home from school with their mother and Robert.

'Dad phoned,' Mrs MacDonald told the twins. 'He has a surprise for you.'

'What is it?' Paul and Sarah asked together, eagerly.

'He went into a large bookshop at lunchtime. He really meant to buy himself a book, but he saw a new book for children. It has most of the stories of the Bible in it and on every page there are coloured pictures, about the stories.'

'It sounds good,' commented Paul.

'May I look at it first?'

'No, Sarah. It's a book you're to share and Dad will decide who looks at it first.'

Robert had heard about the book from Mrs MacDonald after Mr MacDonald had called her on the telephone. He was busy looking around as they walked home.

'What's that?' asked Robert, as he pointed to a large cross in the garden in front of a church. On the cross there was a figure of a man. The cross was made of wood and the man was made of metal.

'That's meant to be like the cross Jesus died on,' explained Paul. 'It's a kind of statue of Jesus.'

Robert looked a little puzzled, but he didn't ask any more questions.

Without telling each other, Paul and Sarah both listened for their father's car stopping outside. At ten to six came the familiar sound.

'There's Dad's car!'

They both rushed to the front door as their father came in.

'Where is it, Dad?'

'Where's what?' replied Mr MacDonald, pretending to be surprised.

'The book.'

'The book?' questioned Mr MacDonald, as if he didn't know what they were talking about.

'Dad, you are a tease!' shouted Sarah.

'All right,' laughed Mr MacDonald. 'After dinner I'll show it to you.'

About half an hour later, Mrs MacDonald exclaimed, 'That's about the fastest dinner you children have eaten for a long time!'

'We want to see the new book,' Sarah explained.

Mr MacDonald sat down on the sofa with Paul, Sarah and Robert.

'Which picture would you like to see first?'

'Jonah and the great fish,' Sarah managed to say first.

There were four pictures about Jonah. There was one of Jonah going into the ship and one of the ship at sea in a tremendous storm. The picture of Jonah washed up on the shore after being in the big fish took up nearly two whole pages. The fourth picture was of the leafy tree which Jonah sat under for shelter when he sulked.

'What can we look at next, Dad?' Paul asked.

'Let Robert choose.'

'Jesus on the cross, please.'

Mr MacDonald turned the pages over until he found the place. The picture took up two pages. On one page there were three crosses, with Jesus hanging on the one in the middle. On the other page were the soldiers. They had Jesus' coat, and they were throwing dice to see who should have it.

'It reminds me of the hymn "There is a Green Hill," Dad.'

'Yes, Sarah. Why don't we sing part of it together.'

And so they sang the first verse.

There is a green hill far away,
Outside a city wall,
Where the dear Lord was crucified
Who died to save us all.'

'Weren't the soldiers cruel and unkind,' Sarah said as she looked at the picture in the book.

Mr MacDonald agreed. 'Yes, they were, but I think if the Lord Jesus lived on earth today people would still treat Him in a similar way.'

'Do you think Jesus knew when He was a boy that He would have to die on the cross?' she asked.

'The Bible doesn't tell us much about that,' answered Mr MacDonald. 'He did know though before He first met Peter and John and all the other disciples. Once the Lord Jesus asked the disciples, "Who do men say that I am?" The disciples told Him that some thought He was John the Baptist, others Elijah, others Jeremiah, or one of the prophets. And then He asked, "Who do you say I am?" Peter answered, "You are the Christ, the Son of the living God."'

'I remember,' Sarah butted in. 'Didn't Jesus tell them then that He was going to die?'

Mr MacDonald nodded. 'The Lord Jesus then told His disciples that He must go to Jerusalem and there suffer at the hands of the Jewish leaders, and that He would be killed. He also told them that after three days He would be raised to life again.'

Sarah thought for a moment and asked, 'But when did Jesus first know that He had to die?'

'When He was very young, I expect,' suggested Paul. 'But He couldn't have known when He was a little baby, could He, Dad? Babies don't know or understand difficult things.'

Mrs MacDonald came into the room and listened to what Paul said.

'You do ask Dad difficult questions!'

'You help me to answer them, Helen.'

'Well,' said Mrs MacDonald, 'I'm sure the Lord Jesus knew when He was a little boy that He was God's Son and that He was going to die on the cross when He was older. But the Bible doesn't tell us when He first knew this. You mustn't forget that He didn't begin His life when He was born into this world: He is God and lives forever. The reason He came into the world was to die on the cross for us.'

'Was Jesus an ordinary baby like the new baby next door?' asked Sarah. 'Did He cry and grow like other children?'

'Yes, I'm sure He did. But although He was like other babies to look at, He was different because He was not only human, He was God as well. As He grew up, He knew He was God's Son. We spoke about this a little the other day.'

'When was that?'

'When I told you about the Lord Jesus going to Jerusalem, Paul. Jesus was not very much older than you are now. He went to Jerusalem for the special services the Jews had in the temple. Mary and Joseph took Him with them. When the feast was over, Mary and Joseph started back for home, but the Lord Jesus stayed in Jerusalem because He wanted to spend more time in the temple. Mary and Joseph didn't know that

He wasn't with them. They thought He was playing with friends in some other part of the crowd going home from Jerusalem. They walked for a whole day without seeing Him. Then they began to look for Him among their friends and relatives.'

'I remember,' said Sarah. 'As they couldn't find Him they went back to Jerusalem to look for Him. After looking for three days, they found Him sitting in the temple with the teachers, listening to them and asking questions.'

'That's right. Everyone who heard the Lord Jesus was surprised at His intelligence and the answers He gave. Mary and Joseph were rather cross with Him because of the trouble they'd had finding Him. Do you remember what He said?'

'Yes. He said, "Didn't you know that I must be about My Father's business?"'

Then Paul understood why his mother had mentioned Jesus' visit to the temple. 'I see now. Jesus knew when He was at least twelve that He was the Son of God, and if He knew that, He knew too that He had come into the world to die for our sins.'

'I should think so,' agreed his mother. 'As

the Lord Jesus grew so did His knowledge of who He was and why He had come. No one had to tell Him that He was God's Son and why He had come. He knew without anyone telling Him.'

Sarah was thoughtful. 'If Jesus knew from the time He was a little boy that He was going to die on the cross, He must have been brave.'

'Yes. And He must love us very much too, Sarah.'

'That picture is in my book,' interrupted Robert.

'What picture, Robert?' asked Mrs MacDonald.

'Jesus in the temple.'

'So it is. You coloured it, didn't you?'

Robert was looking at the picture in the book Mr MacDonald had brought home. It was still open at the picture of Jesus dying on the cross. 'Jesus is still on the cross, isn't He?' he asked.

'Oh, no, Robert,' replied Mrs MacDonald.

'But I saw Him.'

'When?'

'Outside that church.'

Then Mrs MacDonald understood - and

so did the twins. She quickly caught their eye and kept them from laughing at Robert.

'That was only a kind of statue, Robert. The Lord Jesus didn't stay on the cross. They took Him down when they were sure that He had died. But He didn't remain dead. Three days later He came back to life again! Hundreds of people saw Him, and discovered that He's alive. When you see the statue again, remember that the Lord Jesus didn't stay on the cross, but He lives today. It's time for bed now, Robert.'

'Oh, not yet, please. Can we play the game with the matches and the bottle again?'

'Let's!' shouted Paul and Sarah.

'Just for ten minutes then.'

6 Robert discovers the marbles

'What are these?' Robert asked, as he lifted a small plastic bag from the shelf of the bookcase in the living room.

Mrs MacDonald came across the room and looked. 'Oh, they're marbles.'

'What are marbles?'

'They're little balls of glass and you play a game with them.'

'Whose are they?'

'They're Mr MacDonald's actually, Robert. Last Christmas he was given them from the Christmas tree, although he didn't open the bag because we had a young baby staying with us. He didn't want her to play with them and perhaps put one in her mouth. So they were put in the bookcase. I'd forgotten they were still there.'

'Can we play with them?'

Mrs MacDonald smiled. She hadn't played marbles for many years. She could hardly remember how to play.

'All right. Let's count them out.' There were twenty marbles altogether, so Robert and Mrs MacDonald had ten each.

'I'll start by rolling one of mine along the

carpet and then you have to try and roll one of your marbles to hit it. If you hit it, then you win my marble. If you miss, I can try and hit your marble. Every time you hit the other person's marble, it belongs to you. Are you ready to start?'

'Yes,' replied Robert eagerly.

The game began and Robert became very good at hitting Mrs MacDonald's marbles. Mrs MacDonald's knees started to ache from kneeling and Robert rolled his marbles so hard that they often went under the sofa. Mrs MacDonald had to get a long knitting needle to poke them out from underneath.

Suddenly they heard the back door open.

'Is that Paul and Sarah already, Robert?' Mrs MacDonald exclaimed.

The living room door opened and the twins burst in.

'What are you both doing on the floor?'

'We're playing marbles, Sarah,' Mrs MacDonald said laughingly. 'We found the marbles Dad got last Christmas. Robert discovered them in the bookcase.'

'I wondered where they had gone,' Paul said. 'May we have a game?'

'You had better ask Robert, Paul. He won

all my marbles except this one!'

Robert was keen to play again and Paul helped him count out the marbles.

'Sarah can play with me first, if she likes,' Robert offered.

'Thank you, but it's my turn to set the table for dinner and I can't play until I've done that.'

'What kind of day have you had at school, twins?' their mother called from the kitchen.

'Good and bad,' answered Paul.

Mrs MacDonald came and stood in the living room door-way.

'Why was that?'

'Well,' Paul went on to explain, 'it was good because I've been given a place on the football team. I didn't think I was going to get a game. I've been first reserve most of the term. Malcolm has to go away this weekend and so he can't play on Saturday. Mr Trench said I'm to be his substitute. I do hope I play well.'

'You can only do your best, Paul. Dad will be pleased. What was bad about today?'

'Mrs Fox went out of the class-room to get new note-books. Michael Rogers threw a ball across the room. I think he was trying to hit Andrew, but the ball rolled right up to the front of the room. Everyone laughed and made a noise.'

'Did you both laugh as well?'

Paul nodded. 'But that was not the worst. John Foster knew that Mrs Fox would notice the ball and he didn't want Michael to get into trouble. He went to get it and just as he was picking it up - and everyone was talking - Mrs Fox came in. She was very cross. She made him stay after school and help her tidy up. She thought he had caused all the noise.'

'Didn't John tell Mrs Fox that the ball wasn't his?'

'Oh, no. Michael is his friend. Michael knew he ought to get into trouble. But John shook his head when Michael put up his hand to own up. It was decent of John to do that for Michael, wasn't it?'

Mrs MacDonald agreed and she thought for a moment. 'When Dad was talking about the cross last night I wondered how we could help you understand what happened. But I think I can explain now.'

'How, Mum?' Paul enquired.

'When the Lord Jesus died on the cross, He didn't deserve to die. He had never sinned or done anything wrong. But He died in our place, to pay the price of sin. He was our substitute. He took our place, just as Paul will be taking Malcolm's place on Saturday. Malcolm ought to play, but Paul will play instead. We ought to be punished for our sins, but the Lord Jesus died in our place.'

'Were you thinking of John Foster, too?' asked Sarah.

'Yes. Michael did wrong; but John took the punishment. We did wrong; but the Lord Jesus took our punishment on the cross.'

Paul understood it clearly now. 'That's clever of you to put it like that.'

Mrs MacDonald shook her head. 'No, not clever, Paul. The Bible tells us these wonderful things and they are very important.'

****

After dinner Sarah was sitting on the sofa next to her father turning over the pages of the new Bible picture book.

'Look, Dad, there's a picture of the resurrection. Will you tell us about it? You promised to tell us how the resurrection shows that Jesus is God.'

'Yes: but I said when Robert got that far in his painting book.'

Mrs MacDonald explained. 'That will be never then! We had an accident! The paints got knocked over and they went over the book. So we decided to throw it away.'

Robert looked a little ashamed. 'I'm sorry,' he said.

'That doesn't matter, Robert. Come and stand by me and see this picture of the resurrection. Let's look at the picture together. There are the women who went early to the tomb. When they got there, they found it empty. And look, here's another picture. There's the Lord Jesus in the middle of the room, with the disciples standing around Him. All the disciples were there, except Thomas. The resurrection was God saying to everyone, "Jesus is My Son."'

'What do you mean, Dad?' Sarah asked, looking rather puzzled.

'Well, let me ask you some questions. Did the Lord Jesus let people know that He was God before He died?'

Sarah nodded her head.

'Did He really die when He was put on

65

the cross?'

'Yes, Dad.'

'Could any man or woman have given Him life again?'

'Of course not.'

'Who raised Him from the dead, then?'

'God did.'

'Suppose the Lord Jesus hadn't been telling the truth when He said He was God's Son. Do you think God would have then raised Him from the dead?'

'No: I'm sure He wouldn't have, Dad.'

'Well, when God raised Jesus from the dead He was letting everyone know that Jesus is His Son. You imagine a boy at school telling you that his Dad was very important. How would you know?'

Sarah thought for a moment. 'By seeing him with an important man and hearing him speak to him as his son?'

'I see what you mean, Dad,' interrupted Paul. 'Last term one of the boys told us that his dad was high up in the navy. We didn't believe him. But then one day his father was waiting outside school. We could tell he was important by his officer's uniform. This boy ran straight out of school to meet him and I heard the officer say, "Hello, son." I knew then that he'd told us the truth and I told the others.'

'Fine, Paul,' said Mr MacDonald in approval. 'The resurrection was God saying to everyone, "Jesus is My Son". The Lord Jesus appeared to the women, to Peter, and to the disciples. At one time He appeared to more than five hundred Christians together. God wanted them all to be sure that Jesus is His Son. And then God made certain that it was all written down in the Bible so that people like us could be sure too.'

Robert had gone to the bottom shelf of the bookcase again to fetch the marbles.

'Look what I found this afternoon!'

'My marbles!' exclaimed Mr MacDonald. 'Have you been playing with them?'

'Yes. Would you like a game?'

Mr MacDonald smiled. 'I think there's time for a game or two before bed.'

Before long they were playing excitedly and by the time they had played a game each, it was bedtime.

7 Robert's last day

Robert was sharing Paul's bedroom. On Saturday morning he was first to wake up and he thought he would wake Paul.

'Paul. Wake up! It's Saturday morning.'

Paul sat up in bed, not at all sorry that Robert had woken him up.

'I'm glad it's Saturday. No school today and Dad doesn't have to go to work. We can play with you all day.'

'Yes,' agreed Robert, 'and my mummy and daddy are coming home today!'

'I'd forgotten that, Robert. It will seem strange not having you share my bedroom.'

****

On Saturday morning breakfast was later than usual for the MacDonald family and it was half past nine before Paul had eaten his last piece of toast and marmalade. Just as Robert was finishing his corn flakes, Sarah asked him, 'Are you excited, Robert?'

'Mmmm,' nodded Robert. Then after a moment he said, 'I didn't want to talk with

69

my mouth full. I don't want to be a "goop".'

Mr MacDonald laughed. 'Have the twins taught you that poem, Robert? Can you say it on your own?'

Robert wanted to show Mr MacDonald that he could, so he said the piece of funny poetry all through:

> *'The goops they lick their fingers,*
> *And the goops they lick their knives;*
> *They spill their broth on the tablecloth -*
> *Oh, they lead disgusting lives!*
> *The goops they talk while eating,*
> *And loud and fast they chew;*
> *And that is why I'm glad that I*
> *Am not a goop - are you?'*

'Very good. We must all be careful not to be goops. Now, Sarah, would you get the Bibles for our reading, please.'

Sarah went over to the bookshelf to collect the Bibles. She looked at the Bible reading notes to see where the reading was.

'We start reading in the book of Acts today, Dad.'

'Whose turn is it to read?' Mr MacDonald asked.

'Mine, Dad,' answered Paul.

'Right. Please read verses one to eleven in chapter 1. Afterward I'll ask you some questions to see if you've understood.'

Paul read the passage through carefully. At the end Mr MacDonald said, 'Will you read the last three verses again, please.'

So Paul read, 'After He said this, He was taken up before their very eyes, and a cloud hid Him from their sight. They were looking intently up into the sky as He was going, when suddenly two men dressed in white stood beside them. "Men of Galilee," they said, "why do you stand here looking into the sky? This same Jesus, who has been taken from you into heaven, will come back in the same way you have seen Him go into heaven."'

'Ready for questions?'

'Yes, Dad.'

'Where did the Lord Jesus go?'

'Into heaven.'

'Your turn, Paul. What did the angels say to the disciples?'

'They asked them why they stood looking up into heaven.'

'Was that all?'

'No: they said that Jesus would come again just as He left them - or, at least, I think that was what they said.'

'Yes. You are right. Where is the Lord Jesus now, Robert?'

Robert thought for a while before answering, as if he were afraid he might be wrong. Then he asked, 'In heaven?'

'Yes, in heaven.'

'How do you know that there's a place called heaven?' Paul asked.

'Well, the Bible tells us so, and Jesus told us too.'

Sarah had often thought about heaven and she asked, 'What does Jesus do in heaven?'

'The Bible does not tell us much about that. The Lord Jesus said that He went to prepare a place in heaven for all who trust in Him. We know too that He remembers us and helps us when we pray. You're full of questions this morning!'

When Mr MacDonald said this, it made Paul want to ask all the more!

'Will Jesus really come back again, Dad?'

'I'm sure He will. He promised, "I will come again". Can He break a promise?'

'No,' said the twins in unison.

Mr MacDonald went on. 'The early

Christians were sure that the Lord Jesus would come back again. When we meet people we often say, "Good morning" or "Good afternoon." Instead they would say to one another, "The Lord is coming!"'

Paul felt even more inquisitive. 'When will it be, Dad?'

'Ah,' answered Mr MacDonald. 'No one knows except God. No one knows either the day or the hour. It will be unexpected and ever so quick - it will take place as quick as a wink. He will come as suddenly as a burglar robs a house.'

Sarah interrupted. 'A girl in our class said that burglars came to their house.'

'They didn't expect them, did they?'

'Oh, no.'

'The Lord Jesus will come just as suddenly and without people expecting Him.'

'Why doesn't He come now, then?' Paul asked.

'I can give you only part of the answer to that. When Jesus comes it will be too late for people who've not trusted in Him. God is so patient that He gives more and more time. One day though He will say that the world has had enough time; and Jesus will come.'

Sarah shared Paul's inquisitiveness now.

'What's going to happen when Jesus does come?'

'Phew!' exclaimed Mr MacDonald. 'What a lot of questions! Well, first of all, we shall see the Lord Jesus.'

'And then, Dad?'

'The resurrection of the dead will take place.'

'What do you mean?'

'Everyone who has believed in the Lord Jesus will be raised from the dead, like Jesus was. He will give them bodies which are just right for heaven. And they will be bodies which will never become ill or grow old. Christians everywhere - whether they're alive or have died - will be gathered together to heaven. It will be like a farmer collecting all his harvest.'

'Is there any more, Dad?' asked Sarah.

'Well, after this will come the judgment. The Lord Jesus will reward those who have trusted in Him as Saviour and served Him, and He will punish those who have not. Some people will be very happy and others will be sad. But it's time now that we had our prayer, isn't it?'

'One more question, Dad, please,' pleaded Paul. 'What will happen to the world then?'

'The Bible says that in the end the world and all that's in it will be burned up and destroyed, and there will be a new world altogether to take its place.'

'It's exciting, isn't it?'

'Yes, it is, Paul. Let's pray together now, shall we?'

Then Mr MacDonald prayed, thanking God for the Lord Jesus and for the promise that one day He will return.

****

Saturday morning was bright and sunny, but the afternoon was cloudy. It wasn't long before the rain began to pour down.

'Just look at it, Mum. What can we do?' asked Paul.

'Sarah and I had an idea while we were out shopping this morning. We bought some tooth-picks. Here they are.'

'Oh!' exclaimed Paul, with excitement, 'like the ones we had once before when it rained during our holiday at the beach.'

'Yes. You explain to Robert, Paul.'

'You see these thin strips of wood, Robert - they're tooth-picks. We cut up paper into small squares and we colour them like flags. Then we paste the flags carefully to the top of the tooth-picks.' Then Paul stopped. 'Oh, but we haven't any glue left!'

Sarah laughed. 'Oh, yes we have! We thought of that.'

Mrs MacDonald smiled. 'We bought two glue sticks. Robert can have one and you two can share the other. That's if you can share anything without squabbling!'

Paul had an idea. 'I'm going to do what I wanted to do but couldn't when we were away that time at the beach. I think there are pictures of flags in our encyclopaedia. I would like to copy some of them.'

He went to the bookcase and found the volume he was looking for. He quickly found the word 'flags' in the index and turned to the right page.

'Look, Dad!' he cried. 'There are lots and lots of them - hundreds! There are sixteen pages of small flags. I'm going to have fun making some of them.'

Mr MacDonald had not seen the flags in the book and he went across to the table to look at them. 'Terrific, aren't they? It makes me think how wonderful it's going to be one day.'

'What do you mean, Dad?'

'Well, we've been talking about the Lord Jesus' coming again. When He comes, He will gather together His people from every nation - from all the countries that have flags and all those peoples that haven't flags. People from every tribe and nation will be taken to heaven. As you make the flags of the different countries, remember that the Lord Jesus wants people in each of them to believe in Him, so that they may be with Him for ever in heaven when He comes again.'

Robert had already started making his flags. Using his coloured pencils, he made all kinds of patterns. He liked sticking them onto the toothpicks, but he got so much glue on his fingers that when he stuck the flags on the ends of the toothpicks they came off again as he took his fingers away!

Just before dinner time, when they were clearing all their things from the table, the doorbell rang.

'I think it's Mummy and Daddy!' shouted Robert. And it was. Robert was so excited he could not stop jumping up and down.

'Hello, Robert. We're glad to see you!'

'I'm glad to see you too, Mummy.'

'Have you had a good time?'

'Yes, Daddy.'

'We've brought the twins a present each because we're sure they've been kind to you.'

'Have you brought something for me, too?'

His mother smiled and his father laughed. 'Yes, a game.'

'Oh, good!' Robert shouted. 'I've played lots of new games here, Daddy.'

'What kind of games?'

'Putting matchsticks on the top of bottles, marbles, making flags - and, oh, lots of things.'

'You have had a wonderful time.'

'I'd like to come again.'

Mrs MacDonald was glad to hear Robert say this and so were the twins. 'So you shall, Robert. Can't he, twins?'

'Yes, of course,' they agreed enthusiastically.

The Puzzling Book

compiled by
KIRSTI PATERSON
and illustrated by
JANIS MENNIE

The puzzles in this book are based on the New International Version of the Bible.

There are six sections, each containing up to eight puzzles.

An invaluable resource for Sunday School and day-school teachers, as well as teaching vital Bible truths to children in the 10-12 year old age group.

Other puzzle books published by Christian Focus Publications include:

CHRISTIAN ARMOUR
DANIEL AND HIS THREE FRIENDS
DAVID AND GOLIATH
MOSES
NOAH'S ARK
THE NAMES OF JESUS
PEOPLE JESUS MET